i will still be whole
(when you rip me in half)

Ava Wong Davies

i will still be whole
(when you rip me in half)

OBERON BOOKS
LONDON

WWW.OBERONBOOKS.COM

First published in 2019 by Oberon Books Ltd
521 Caledonian Road, London N7 9RH
Tel: +44 (0) 20 7607 3637 / Fax: +44 (0) 20 7607 3629
e-mail: info@oberonbooks.com
www.oberonbooks.com

PB ISBN: 9781786829276
E ISBN: 9781786829269

Cover image © Xiao Lu

Printed and bound by 4EDGE Limited, Hockley, Essex, UK.
eBook conversion by Lapiz Digital Services, India.

Visit www.oberonbooks.com to read more about all our books and to buy them. You
will also find features, author interviews and news of any author events, and you can
sign up for e-newsletters and be the first to hear about our new releases.

Printed on FSC accredited paper

10 9 8 7 6 5 4 3 2 1

For my parents

Acknowledgements

This play would not exist were it not for the following people.

To Helen Morley – the most sensitive and empathetic director/partner-in-crime I could ever hope to work alongside. Thank you for pushing me when I needed to be pushed, for picking me up and dusting me off when I was down, and having such unwavering faith in this story from its very messy beginnings. You're a dream.

To Emily Davis – the hardest-working person I know. You're simply the best. Thank you for coming on when you did, for pushing us to apply to VAULT in the first place, for writing innumerable applications, for always being calm and collected in a crisis. For dealing with our (my) bullshit with a firm yet loving practicality. There would be no show without you.

To Aoife Hinds and Tuyen Do – thank you for your generosity and playfulness, for your time and your patience. And to Rosa Escoda and Kailing Fu, our OG duo – your help in developing, realising, and embodying these two women was completely invaluable.

To Clara Potter-Sweet, Jordan Rice, Ben Kulvichit, Grace Venning, Jamie King-Cox, Zara Janmohamed, Amanda Fleming – I can't thank you enough for all the work and effort you put into making this show bigger and better than I could ever imagine. I am floored by your talent, hard work, and creativity.

To Xiao Lu, whose art has inspired us from the very beginning. Thank you for giving us permission to use your work.

To all the people who have shown me and this play encouragement and kindness over the last two years – Lara Tysseling and The Yard, Georgie Straight and Will Adolphy, Emma Blackman and Theatre Deli, Lynette Linton, Emma Noelle Clark, Lilian Tsang, Gill Greer and VAULT Festival, Ross Hunter, Lulu Raczka, Alice Birch, Daniel York Loh, Stewart Pringle, Grace Gummer, Matt Maltby, Jessi Stewart, Serena Grasso and Oberon, Wei Ming Kam, Prime Theatre, Broccoli Arts and the whole *Before I Was A Bear* team, and of course Chris Sonnex, David Ralf, and everyone at The Bunker – thank you all.

To my friends – for showing up and showing out, for giving it (and me) your time, your love, and your energy. Thank you.

And to my family – for whom this is for, and without whom none of this would ever have been possible. I'm so grateful for your constant love and support.

i will still be whole (when you rip me in half) was first performed at VAULT Festival on 27 February 2019 with Kailing Fu as Joy and Rosa Escoda as EJ. It then transferred to The Bunker Theatre on 12 November 2019. Cast and crew were as follows:

TUYEN DO – Joy

Credits include: *Kings of Hell's Palace* (Hampstead Theatre); *Pah-La* (Royal Court); *The Great Wave* (National Theatre); *Enola Holmes* (Legendary Pictures).

AOIFE HINDS – EJ

Credits include: *Normal People* (BBC/Hulu); *Derry Girls* (Channel 4); *The Feed* (Amazon).

AVA WONG DAVIES – Writer

Ava Wong Davies is a playwright and theatre critic based in London. As an arts writer, she is a regular contributor to *Exeunt Magazine* and *The Stage*, and is a monthly columnist for *gal-dem*. As a playwright, her work has been showcased at The Yard, The Bunker, Theatre Deli, the North Wall, and VAULTS Festival. She was a member of the Soho Theatre Writers Lab 18-19, and is currently part of the Bush Theatre's Emerging Writers Group.

HELEN MORLEY – Director

Helen Morley is a theatre director and facilitator interested in developing new work that is formally playful and socially engaged. She has collaborated with Ava on *i will still be whole (when you rip me in half)* since its very first iteration in 2017. She is the current Young Director at Prime Theatre in Swindon, making work for and by young people in schools, community and youth theatre settings.

EMILY DAVIS – Producer

Emily Davis is a theatre producer from Somerset, specialising in devised and experimental performance. She regularly collaborates with Emergency Chorus, This Noise and Poltergeist theatre companies. She also writes criticism for *Exeunt Magazine*, and works as a theatre administrator at Farnham Maltings.

GRACE VENNING – Designer

Grace is a performance designer from London. She was a resident design assistant at the National Theatre from 2018 to 2019. In 2019 she was a finalist for the JMK Award with Jocelyn Cox, and for the inaugural Naomi Wilkinson Award for Stage Design with *Told by an Idiot*. She graduated with a First Class BA (Hons) in Design for Performance from the Royal Welsh College of Music and Drama in 2017.

Design credits include: *If Not Now, When* (National Theatre: Dorfman); *Before I Was a Bear, FCUK'D* (Bunker Theatre); *Time of Listening* (Snape Maltings); *Opera Scenes* (Guildhall School of Music and Drama); *La bohème* (Clonter Opera); *Semele* (Mid Wales Opera tour); *The Death of Ivan Ilyich* (Attic Theatre Co.); Stop *Giving Me Grief* (from the Forest Festival); *Masti Maja* (Sansaar Theatre Co.); *The cosmonaut's last message to the woman he once loved in the former Soviet Union*; *Road* (Bute Theatre, RWCMD).

CLARA POTTER-SWEET – Dramaturg

Clara Potter-Sweet is a dramaturg and theatre-maker from London, making and collaborating on experimental performance. She is co-founder of award-winning theatre company Emergency Chorus ('Beguiling and enchanting work', *The Guardian*) with Ben Kulvichit and Emily Davis. She has shown work and performed at venues including the Lyric Hammersmith, New Diorama, The Yard and Theatr Clwyd. Other collaborations include: The Wardrobe Ensemble, Anna Himali Howard & why this sky.

JORDAN RICE – Sound Designer

Jordan Rice is a writer, director, and sound designer. They have released several independent projects online, from the ambient and dreamy, to harsher, more experimental pieces. Their sounds have been featured in Ralph Sepe Jr.'s film *Lover*, and have seen the stage in pieces such as Lamplit's 2017 Edinburgh Fringe show, *Roaming Collisions*. Jordan co-wrote and directed the sketch comedy show *That's So GCSE* for the 2018 Edinburgh Fringe Festival, with their theatre company Good Bad Ideas.

BEN KULVICHIT – Lighting Designer

Ben is a theatre-maker and co-artistic director of award-winning company Emergency Chorus. As lighting designer, his previous credits include *Portents* (The Space Arts Centre) and *i will still be whole (when you rip me in half)* (VAULT Festival).

ZARA JANMOHAMED – Stage Manager

Recent work has included – Production Management: *Germ Free Adolescent* (Bunker Theatre); *We Anchor In Hope* (Bunker Theatre, Edinburgh Fringe/Mick Perrin Worldwide, Shakespeare UK and European Tour, RADA Festival); *Dramatic Dining Cabaret* and *Rotterdam* (RADA); *Fuck You Pay Me, Box Clever/Killymuck* and *GROTTY* (Bunker); *The Amber Trap* (Theatre503); *Hoard, Sitting* and *Mrs Dalloway* (Arcola).

Stage Management: *Dick Whittington and his Cat* (Oxford Playhouse); *80th Anniversary Gala* (Oxford Playhouse); *A Passage To India* (Tour/Park); *Raising Martha* (Park); *Scapegoat* (St Stevens Church) and *Kill Me Now* (Park).

JAMIE KING-COX – Production Manager

As a freelance technician, Jamie has worked at VAULTS Festival, Garsington Opera and Edinburgh Fringe with Underbelly in the last year, as well as various lighting programming and rigging work in the South East. He is also useful to have around, as being the tall one, he is able to reach anything on high shelves.

Characters

JOY
40s – Chinese

EJ
20s – Chinese/White

Notes

'	suggests a silence
[square brackets]	indicates an unsaid thought
/	suggests a point of interruption

Words should slip off without any reverence towards the poetics. Resist the urge to lean into the heightened lyricism.

PRELUDE

JOY   Look through the window of this small house in Shepherd's Bush.

It is four a.m. on a Tuesday.

Look through the window.

There's a young woman with thick black hair.

She's leaning over a powder-blue crib. One with satin ribboning.

EJ   The baby in the crib is tiny.

Weeks old.

JOY   She cries.

EJ   She cries.

JOY   A lot.

EJ   Yes.

She's a baby.

JOY   The woman leaning over the crib has rounded, pink cheeks.

EJ   Remnants of her childhood.

JOY   And she's startlingly quiet.

EJ   Startlingly still.

You can almost see the vines creeping up her legs.

Through the window, the uppermost branches of a peach tree quiver.

JOY   Her eyes flicker up to it.

EJ   She doesn't try to calm the baby.

JOY   A woman made out of marble.

EJ	So baby screams. Logically.
	It reaches up and waves tiny fists.
	Twisting its little red mouth.
	And the young woman still does nothing but look.
JOY	She can't do anything but look.
EJ	She could.
JOY	Her husband is in the next room.
	He lies, spread-eagled.
	He stirs, mouth open, and licks his lips, but doesn't wake up.
	The woman isn't thinking about him.
	The woman stares down at the baby.
EJ	Her baby.
JOY	The woman stares down at her baby –
	At its soft skull.
	She imagines cupping its Play-Doh head in her hands and pressing down.
	She imagines leaving two thumbprint-sized dents in its skull.
EJ	She's scared.
JOY	No.
EJ	She is.
JOY	She's not scared – she's –
	Curious.
EJ	There's a bag lying at her feet.

2

JOY	Almost despite herself, she begins to coo and shush.
EJ	And the baby opens its eyes and stares up at her face and stops crying.
JOY	And they look at each other for a brief moment.
EJ	The baby smiles.
JOY	The young woman smiles.
EJ	And then?
JOY	And then.
	And then the young woman looks away.
	She looks at the bag at her feet.
EJ	And.
JOY	And the stone which encased her body cracks open.
	And she shakes off the vines and the dust.
	And she feels the blood beneath her skin.
	And she picks up the bag and she walks out of the room and she doesn't look back.
EJ	Yes.
	And the baby?
JOY	I don't know.
	'
EJ	The baby lies on her back and the smile slips off her face and she begins to cry again.
	And somewhere in the early morning a door shuts.
	And a latch clicks.
	And the young woman is gone.

3

PART ONE

EJ   She kisses like a cannibal.

Her hair is rough. Straw-like through fingers.

There's a cut on her bottom lip.

I feel it under my tongue.

It is shockingly hot in here.

Skin radiating.

Air close.

It's difficult to breathe deeply.

I wonder what she does for a living.

When she's not in basement clubs at four thirty-two a.m. on Thursday nights I wonder what she does with herself.

Slide my tongue under hers.

Fits perfectly.

The room throbs around us.

Pulsing underwater.

Flashes of skin under blue lights.

Teeth bright and white, bared.

Air hot in throats.

Eyes heavy-lidded.

Bodies twist into one.

Small hands knot at the base of my neck.

She's blonde.

She's probably in PR.

4

She has blue eyes.

Bright, bright blue eyes.

Bright, bright blonde hair.

She has the look of a girl who'd be good at baking apple crumbles for her family on the weekend.

Hands grasp the top of my shoulders.

Skin scalds.

When I walked in she gave me a look from across the room.

The first person I saw.

There was a line of sweat on her lip and I thought about wiping it off with the tip of my finger and there was a tug –

Just –

Here.

She gestures to the bottom of her abdomen.

> She tucked straw-like hair behind her ears and smiled at me and I –
>
> Just –
>
> Smiled –
>
> Back.
>
> These kisses are volcanic.
>
> She told me her name –
>
> Something like
>
> Lara –
>
> Or –

Anna –

Or –

Alice.

I unstick my body from hers.

Bruises bloom under my lips.

She stares at me.

Blue eyes blazing.

She's saying something.

I tilt my head.

Her mouth a soft pink smudge.

I want to put my index finger on her bottom lip.

'

Sometimes I feel like my head is floating two inches above my body.

Sometimes I think there's a metre between my skin and my organs.

'

And then all these blurred bodies snap back into crisp-cut lines and sound rushes in like it's been squeezed out of a vacuum.

She wants me to go home with her.

JOY   The egg hits the pan with a hot crack and the edges, milky clear, start to thicken.

A fox screams somewhere and I turn.

My kitchen sink faces onto a window.

And my window faces onto a small garden.

My garden.

Mostly weeds and brambles.

Wildflowers peering through the chaos.

I like it that way.

I like the feeling of thorns raking my ankles.

The perimeter of the sky is a curdled blue. Slightly hazed just above the trees.

It is still dark enough that I can see my face in the glass.

It's ghostly.

Swimming distorted in frame.

Slightly sickly under the eyes.

That's genetic.

It doesn't matter how much sleep I get.

There is a soft, tired ache embedded deep in my temples.

I gently press my middle and index fingers into the blue hollows.

The egg splutters and coughs on the stove.

I unstick it.

It grumbles.

My mother made me fried eggs when I couldn't sleep.

Just one.

Perfectly formed, every time.

Slipped into a china bowl, dripped with soy sauce, eaten with a spoon.

Salty soft.

When I had to pump in the middle of the night I'd make them.

I can crack an egg with one hand without even looking.

That's my party trick.

The yolk quivers.

I think about bursting it.

The pan spits oil onto my thumb.

EJ   Wrists plunged under the tap.

Face hot.

Feverish.

Splashing water onto cheeks like they do in films.

Music bubbles from underneath the door.

Bathroom lights are cold.

Flattening.

Look into the mirror –

And –

And –

And –

A blur.

Grip the sides of the sink.

Lean forward.

Nose tip touches glass.

Squint.

A pale orb –

Right at the centre of the mirror.

Tap it with a finger.

Twice.

Nothing.

Trace the outline with a nail.

Nothing.

Breath rises.

Eyes squeeze shut.

'

A peach tree crawling up a stone wall.

Count each branch.

See it bloom in fast-forward.

Damp earth under soft bare feet. Petals crushed into a fist.

And the smell?

Nothing.

'

I take the soft skin on the inside of my elbow, twist and pinch hard.

I do it again –

And again –

And again –

Until the skin is puckered pink.

I should go with her.

The bathroom door bangs.

A flash of straw-like hair.

Hot air rushes in.

Music booms.

Bright, bright blue eyes.

Two pricks of red on each cheek.

A film of sweat glittering on her brow.

There is a really levelling smell of old piss in here.

Her lips open –

And –

I rush forward to kiss her open mouth.

Or –

I smack her head into the sink and watch a cut open up in the perfect paleness of her cheek.

Or –

'I'm sorry.'

I say it before I mean it.

Blue eyes glassy clear.

I run.

JOY   I eat the egg straight out of the pan.

I eat it in thirty seconds flat, and then I wash up, dry, and put the pan back in the kitchen cupboard.

I wipe down the counter and put away the cloth.

I take the cloth out again and spritz the counter with disinfectant and wipe it down one more time.

I think about descaling the kettle.

I open the backdoor and stand in the garden, weeds curling around my feet.

She pauses, considering. Then –

When I was full with you it was the summer and I spent so many hours lying on my back, gasping like an ox.

You strained against me.

I didn't glow in pregnancy.

I sallowed.

You didn't sleep.

You kicked –

Constantly.

And I would lie there with my fists held to my eyes.

But I wouldn't cry.

You could never get me to cry.

He lay next to me.

Spread-eagled.

One arm thrown over my chest.

A nuclear snorer.

The drapes in the room were corpse-heavy. We'd go around with tea towels tied over our mouths, beating them with wooden spoons.

When I couldn't sleep I'd go downstairs and lift the latch and walk onto the grass.

Brambles up to my thighs and nettles grazing my shins.

The air there.

11

The air was clear.

I could breathe again.

At the very back of the garden there was a tree with dark sweeping branches which rested very slightly against a stone wall and that tree, in the month you were born, unfurled for me and dropped blushed velvet peaches into my lap.

They weren't sweet.

They were stubbornly hard.

The white ones my mother cut into segments were sweeter, more delicate.

But these were something, still.

EJ   Fox.

Right there.

Right in front of me.

We both freeze.

Cool, yellow-eyed stare.

It grips an old KFC box in its jaws.

A rivulet of spit drips from black lips.

I crouch.

We are three feet away from each other.

In the middle of a road.

A nice residential road.

This fox has ripped a full bin bag to shreds.

Strewn the contents over a manicured little street.

Rolled around in it.

Picked off the best bits.

Left the rest to rot.

I crouch and put my hands flat on the ground.

I have never been this close to a fox before.

I like them.

I try not to blink.

It shifts its weight, but holds the gaze.

Don't blink.

One –

Two –

Three –

Still.

Four –

Five –

Six –

And then –

I hold out both my hands.

I don't know why.

Palms up.

And I swear its eyes narrow.

Seven –

Eight –

It turns its head.

Nine –

It sniffs the dawn air.

Looks back at me.

Decidedly uninterested now.

Then it trots away.

My hands, still upturned in offering.

I get to my feet.

I feel stupid.

Stupid. Stupid.

I watch it hurry down the street and turn into an alleyway.

It doesn't look back.

Why would it?

'

Shame.

I could've used a friend.

JOY   I couldn't sleep for years afterwards.

You clung on.

My body twisted for you. Ached.

I needed to purge you.

I drank a lot and I ate a lot and neither filled the hole and there just became more of me to fill and less of you to do it.

I started to run.

In the mornings, in the evenings.

Whenever I could.

And –

Not away from you.

Just –

Towards myself.

EJ   I have such an urge to lie down in the middle of the road.

Like they do in *The Notebook*.

But it looks stupid if you're not doing it with someone you want to sleep with so I don't.

I keep walking.

I wonder if she's gone home now. If she'll think of me before she falls asleep tonight. This morning. If she'll think of me in the shower. On the tube on her commute, with her legs crossed, vibrations crawling up her skirt.

'

I walk.

And I walk.

And I walk.

JOY   This city was not built for me.

The buildings used to arc away.

Shying out of my path.

Steel curving.

Screaming with the effort.

I was invisible for so long.

Quiet, passive, amenable.

People looked over me.

At the spot just above my head.

Gazes flitted past.

People don't like to look at women like you and me.

Only when it suits them.

If they had it their way –

They'd swallow us up.

Compress us.

Tuck us away.

These translucent women.

'

Watch me solidify.

I carve out my own city.

Houses topple in my path.

I step over shattered glass and dusted brick.

Leap over bridges and rivers without a gasp.

Bat away putty-pink people with the back of my hand.

With every step –

The ground trembles.

Faces upturn and stare in awe and I rumble past.

I sweat.

A lot.

I let it run down my forehead, matt my hair, nestle
into the hollow of my clavicle.

I have earned it.

Every straining muscle.

Every last one.

I rise in the distance, the edges of myself becoming crisper each day.

And you –

I think of you –

A reasonable amount.

A kind amount.

But doesn't feel like my heart has been pulled out of my throat.

'

I don't know if it ever felt like that.

The light –

EJ   The light is rising.

Spilling out from behind chimneys.

I should've gone home with her.

She smelled like cocoa butter and sweat.

Dark blue diluting into a milky lavender.

There's a faint crackling in the air.

Like TV static.

And a low hiss. Air escaping from a tyre.

I can feel it on my skin. Raising the hairs on my arms.

Smells electric.

‘

There's a house at the end of the street.

JOY   I make friends quickly.

Afterwards.

We go to the pub.

A lot. We go to the pub all the time.

We have dinner parties.

One night I cook them noodles and they can't finish it for the tears streaming down their faces.

I stop cooking Chinese food.

I feel the weight of Cantonese on my tongue.

Pulling me down.

EJ   A house at the end of the street.

JOY   I practice in the mirror until my eyelids droop.

Tongue curling around vowels.

Spaces open up.

People smile when they hear my perfect, accentless voice.

Particularly men.

With big shining teeth.

Men smile at me –

A lot.

EJ   Something isn't right.

JOY   I smile back.

EJ   There's a house at the end of the street and I think –

Something isn't right.

The sky behind it is stained red.

In the windows, behind the shutters, there is an orange haze.

There are sirens wailing in the distance.

I'm standing in front of this house and this house is on fire and –

I cannot move –

I cannot move –

I cannot move.

But my chest isn't tight, my chest is loose and open.

And I watch a woman in a dressing gown run out of the front door holding something in a blanket.

And I watch a fire engine screech to a halt metres away from me.

And I watch smoke curl out of the windows of this house and my eyes begin to stream.

There's a baby in the blanket.

It starts to cry.

Did you ever feel like this?

Like your body was trying to hurt you?

JOY   They don't scare me anymore.

       Nothing scares me anymore.

EJ   There's a coil somewhere deep in my abdomen and I
       feel it unfurling.

       My mouth is dry and my eyes are wide.

       The woman is weeping.

       Did I do this?

       Did I make this happen?

*An interlude. Mainly wordless, communicated through look and
touch. It's about dependency and trust, but also control. Most likely an
escalation.*

JOY   It takes twenty-seven days for your skin cells to regenerate.

       Four months for red blood cells.

       Bones take ten years.

       Your brain stays the same.

       Obviously.

       But every twenty-seven days –

       Your skin sheds and stretches anew.

       For a moment, fresh and delicate as a blossom petal
       before it wears away again.

       His touch lingered afterwards.

       It burnt through my skin and crawled right into my nerves.

       If you ran an ultraviolet light over my body I'd light
       up like a Christmas tree.

Fluorescent finger stains everywhere.

I scrub my legs until the skin is sore.

Water runs over me.

He was oppressively obsessive.

Overwhelmed to be allowed near my body.

Couldn't believe his luck.

Quickly became jealous.

Of course.

Inevitably.

He had that in him.

A handsome man with shadowed eyes.

He'd sweep an arm over me.

Hurry me inside.

Cover my bare shoulders.

I was fourteen weeks along and still vomiting.

Constantly.

Without pause.

Worse than it was at six –

Worse than it was at eight.

Anything I ate tasted of bile.

Water was poisonous.

My knees buckled underneath me.

He'd lay me down in that musty room.

Flat on my back.

Staring at a dark ceiling.

And if I tried to speak the bitterness rose up in my throat.

So I closed my mouth and lay mute.

I lay there for hours, head turned on the pillow, staring out of the window.

You can see the uppermost branches of the tree from that room.

I lay there for hours and then for days and then for weeks.

My hair lengthened to my ankles.

My skin shed itself and regrew.

My eyes grew milky.

Ivy curled over my thighs.

His food festered inside me.

I could feel –

You.

Sapping everything out of me.

You had my body.

More and more you occupied my mind.

You sat, heavy and sour, in the darkest corners.

What else could I give you?

EJ   Smoke clings to the ends of my hair.

I can feel it, thin and papery on my fingertips.

Yellow light crawls through the curtains.

I hesitate, hand on doorframe, clutching keys like a hand.

The TV flickers on mute.

A young family are being shown around a run-down semi-detached.

The woman hitches her toddler up onto her hip and grimaces at the mildewed bathroom.

He stirs in his collapsed armchair.

'Dad.'

His eyelids flutter.

'Have you been here all night?'

Something which could pass for a nod.

'Why didn't you go to bed?'

'I did.'

Morning voice like a bullfrog.

I walk over the crunchy carpet.

I kneel at his feet.

Start to untie his laces.

'Why didn't you take off your shoes?'

'I was reading and I fell asleep.'

He yawns stunted yellow teeth. Places a hand on my hair.

'Did you have a nice time?'

The couple on screen are arguing silently. The toddler trembles as the woman waves her hand.

'I'm sorry I wasn't here.'

'Are you working today?'

The woman tears her hand out of the man's and storms out of the damp little semi-detached.

I ball his socks up and put them in my pocket.

'That's better,' I say.

He rubs his eyes.

I rock back onto my heels.

I try to find myself in his face.

Maybe it's somewhere in the mouth.

The lines around the eyes aren't mine.

The tanned, leathery skin isn't mine.

Somewhere in the mouth, I think.

'Help me up.'

I take his elbows. He creaks out of the chair.

He starts towards the kitchen and I reach for his arm.

He waves me away.

'Dad, I'm.'

I stop. He isn't looking back at me.

I have a photo of you saved on my phone in my back pocket.

Hair tied back neatly, mouth a tight, thin line.

Maybe it's my imagination but I swear your lips are curled at the edges.

Like you're holding back a laugh.

You looked younger than I thought you would.

I zoomed in until it was just pixels.

Trying to find myself somewhere in your face.

Proof.

Mouth? No. That's Dad's. Nose? Maybe. Eyes?
Definitely.

I find it so strange that I came out of your body.

That has to – that does something to a person.
Doesn't it?

I open my mouth and then close it again.

The words would be thick on my tongue.

Sometimes when he's drunk he'll go stormy quiet
and beet-red and I know he's thinking about you.

I go to open the curtains and dust settles on my hands.

The window is steamed and I wipe it down.

The tree squats at the back of the garden, glossy-slick
with dew.

I can see the buds from here, clustered velvet on the
branches.

JOY   I quit my job.

        He insisted.

        Suggested.

        Arms encircling me.

        It's what's best for you.

        What's best for her.

        Just relax.

        He'll take care of it.

He called up the supermarket on my behalf.

Always so thoughtful.

She won't be coming in anymore.

At least not until the baby comes.

And then –

Well –

We'll just have to play it by ear.

See how she feels.

No, no.

She's lying down.

She can't come to the phone.

She's doing fine.

Yes.

She's very excited.

EJ   The bath is scalding.

I watch the blood rise to the top of my skin.

I turn on the hot tap as high as it will go.

Five minute intervals, then another blast.

I think this is how they kill lobsters.

JOY   You found me fairly easily.

I think.

I didn't change my name.

I melted away for a while.

Became invisible.

Only temporarily.

I wasn't afraid of him.

He had you.

He adored you.

I yellowed at the edges, curled up, slipped away.

'

You were going to look for me one day.

If you didn't I'd be –

A bit offended.

Probably.

It was an email in my inbox on a Monday morning.

Nothing special.

No teary phone call.

You didn't show up at the office with tears streaming down your face, clutching daffodils.

It was an email and the subject line was –

'(No Subject)'.

EJ   I lie in the bath and I try to let my legs and arms float and I wonder how much it would cost to have a go in a flotation tank.

I think about my skin splitting open.

Pink and red and shining and beautiful.

JOY   And I could tell you that my heart missed a beat and my palms began to sweat and tears rose to my eyes but that would be an exaggeration.

I think –

I think I grasped my mug a little harder.

Tucked a strand of hair behind my ear.

Clicked on it immediately.

But that was about it, really.

No twinge in my abdomen.

My womb didn't ache –

Didn't call out to you like a fleshy homing device.

Nothing like that.

EJ   I wonder if she's asleep. I wonder if she found another girl to go home with. I wonder if they're lying in bed together, legs twisted over each other, morning sun spilling over bare skin.

I look at my own body.

Under the water, my fingers bloom.

I think about the water slipping through my pores until I'm bloated and swollen and stubbornly pink, until someone cuts the string and I float into the ceiling.

There is a patch of black mould almost directly above my head which has been in this house since the day I moved back in.

Six months.

It's gotten bigger.

Dad tells me that I brought it here.

That he's never had mould before, not in this house.

It pulses between mustard tiles.

A little alien baby.

I stare up at it.

I wonder if I'm breathing in the spores.

Little spores crawling down my throat and settling into the warm pinkness of my lungs.

Black flowers blooming there.

We're meeting in a few hours.

I'll be late.

I know it.

But you'll wait.

You owe me that.

You'll wait.

I want to steam my face and open up every pore.

I want to shave off all my body hair and rinse it down the sink.

Pour oil on my body and set myself on fire.

I wonder –

Will any part of me shock you?

Another wordless interlude. Again, about dependency and control. And again, it should not be a break, a moment of breath. It must escalate the situation.

PART TWO

This part should be disorientating. It should resist closure. It should feel disjointed and strange. They should approach each other like wildcats – wary, afraid, but curious too.

'

JOY   I'm sorry.

       I'm sorry.

       I –

       I ran.

       '

EJ   You're sweating.

JOY   I –

       Yes.

       Yes.

EJ   It's okay –

       It's really fine –

       Don't worry about it.

JOY   Buses –

       Diversions –

       You know.

EJ   Yeah –

       No –

       It's –

       It's the worst.

I get it.

JOY   There was a man on a bicycle and the driver didn't see him –

Something / like that

EJ   Right, yeah.

JOY   And they got into an argument.

So there was that, too.

It was really –

Really annoying.

He stopped the bus.

Turned off the engine.

Waving his arms.

The cyclist said he was going to sue.

And –

I was ringing the bell but –

'

So I had to run.

So –

Sweat.

EJ   Yeah.

No it's fine.

Like I said –

It's not a problem.

'

You're really [sweating] –

31

Do you / want some water

JOY   I might get some water.

EJ   Yes.

JOY   Yes.

       I'll get it.

       Do you [want anything?]

EJ   No.

       No.

       Thanks.

JOY   Okay.

She goes and gets it. EJ doesn't know what to do with herself. JOY comes back. She offers EJ the water wordlessly. EJ shakes her head. JOY downs a whole bottle/glass. EJ watches.

       Okay.

       Thanks.

EJ   Sure.

JOY   Shall we sit down?

EJ   Yeah.

They should not sit down.

           '

       Are we going to talk about the weather?

JOY   Well –

       If you like.

EJ   No –

32

No no no.

I'm good.

They smile at each other.

JOY   I haven't introduced myself.

       '

       I know it's silly.

       Ridiculous.

       I know who you are and I know you know [who
       I am] –

       But –

       I'm Joy.

EJ   EJ.

JOY   EJ.

EJ   Yeah.

JOY   You don't go by / Esther

EJ   No –

       Er –

       No.

       I don't –

       Don't love that / name

JOY   Oh, right.

EJ   Sorry –

       No –

       No offence.

It's just –

Sorry.

I don't know.

It's a bit of an old lady name.

I think.

JOY   My mother's English name was Esther.

She chose it for herself.

So that's why I –

That's why you're called [Esther] –

EJ   Right.

Yeah.

JOY   I chose Joy.

Obviously.

EJ   Yeah I don't really have any –

Opinions.

On that.

'

Sorry.

JOY   No –

It's alright.

It's alright.

'

They hold the pause. Maybe they smile awkwardly. Neither knows what to say or do. EJ suddenly comes out with an 'argh' sound. Inexpressible and weird. Maybe it comes out physically too.

JOY   Are you [okay] –

EJ   I don't –

It's all just a bit –

Like –

Argh.

You know?

'

JOY   I –

I don't [know] –

EJ   No –

It doesn't matter –

Sorry.

JOY   Okay.

'

EJ   No, you know what I mean –

Right –

Like –

This is all a bit –

Argh.

Maybe she makes some kind of movement to go along with it.

No?

JOY   I –

Sure.

Yes.

Argh.

Maybe she mirrors the movement.

'

EJ   Right –

        Yeah –

        Exactly.

JOY   Exactly.

        '

        Are you studying?

EJ   I –

        No.

        Not anymore.

        I left last year.

JOY   Left?

EJ   Yes.

        '

JOY   Okay.

        So you're working now?

EJ   I'm a temp.

JOY   Oh –

        Great.

EJ   I mean –

        It's not.

        It's shit.

JOY   Okay.

EJ   It's so bad.

       It's honestly –

       Like –

       I don't know what I'm doing.

       Or why I'm doing it.

       I go to work and I sit at a computer and I stare at the
       screen and I hope no one fires me.

       And then I go home.

       Back to Dad's.

       And I eat toast and we watch *Grand Designs*.

       And I run him a bath.

       And I help him weed the garden.

       And then I take a sleeping pill and go to bed.

       And then I wake up and it starts again.

JOY   I worked as a temp for a while.

EJ   Oh.

JOY   Receptionist.

EJ   Oh right.

JOY   It was in Canary Wharf.

       In a bank.

EJ   Oh right.

       Yeah.

       No, I don't do that.

       No.

       I don't work for a bank.

JOY	No.
EJ	No.
JOY	Who do you work for?
EJ	I wouldn't work for a bank.
	Personally.
	If it were up to me.
	Which it is.
	I just think it's –
	A bit –
	I dunno.
	'
	Unethical.
	I guess.
JOY	I think that's a bit childish.
	'
EJ	Yeah.
	Fine.
	'
	You're shorter.
	Than I thought you would be.
	You look really different to your picture.
	I didn't even recognise you when you walked in.
JOY	I recognised you.
EJ	Right.

Very good.

Well done.

'

He's fine.

By the way.

JOY   You live with him?

EJ   What?

JOY   You said you go home / and see him

EJ   Yeah.

Yes.

Just for a bit.

Just to get him back on his feet.

'

He had –

It's fine.

It's fine.

But he had a stroke.

A small one.

About a year ago.

'

He's fine.

He just needed a bit of help.

But I'll be moving out soon.

As soon as I can afford it.

JOY	That's good of you –
	To stay with him.
	Very Chinese.

EJ	Yeah.
	Well.
	No one else was gonna [do it] –
	There is no one [else] –
	Anyway.
	It's fine.
	'
	Are you [married]?
	'

| JOY | Am I? |
| | What? |

EJ	No.
	Nothing.
	'

JOY	I always hated that house.
	So dark.
	And cold.
	'
	I liked the garden.
	The tree.
	The garden was always beautiful.

Overgrown.

I liked it that way.

EJ   Yeah.

JOY   I used to lie in that main bedroom when I was
        p[regnant] –

        With –

        You.

        And the bed was against the wall opposite the door.

EJ   Yeah.

JOY   And I think that's where the plumbing must've –
        because I would lie there at night with my head
        against the wall and I could hear the pipes rattling.

        Like the house was alive.

        And it always made me feel –

EJ   Like you were going mad.

        That's my bedroom now.

        I think I probably [lie where you used to lie] –

        The pipes tick.

        It's horrible.

        '

        I –

        I know it's [silly] –

        You should –

        I think he'd like to see you.

        If you wanted to come for dinner I could –

41

You don't need to be worried about him.

He would be fine with it.

He isn't –

He's just –

He's just an old man.

JOY That's very kind of you.

EJ If we went back now you could help me cook.

Or I could just cook –

For you.

'

JOY I'm sorry.

EJ Yeah.

Yeah.

No, of course.

Another day, then.

But –

You should see the house.

I've been trying to clean it up.

Make it more of a home.

I repainted the kitchen last week.

It's brighter now.

Fresher.

And the garden – do you remember the garden?

I cleared out the weeds.

And the brambles –

And nettles –

And ivy.

I pruned the tree.

It's starting to blossom.

And –

And it'll bear fruit in the summer.

Hopefully.

I was going to go and pick up some flowers for planting this weekend.

We could go together.

If you wanted.

I don't really know anything about flowers, do you?

'

JOY No.

Not much.

EJ Yeah.

That's a shame.

'

Why'd you leave?

'

JOY I –

What?

EJ Why'd you leave?

'

I'm fucking with you.

'

JOY	That's not [funny] –
	That isn't –
	Wasn't –
EJ	Funny?
JOY	No.
	It wasn't funny.
EJ	I thought it was quite funny.
	I thought it was really funny, actually.

'

JOY	Do you want me to tell you?
EJ	Do you even know?
JOY	I can tell you.
	If you want to know.
EJ	Was it him?
JOY	It was me.

'

EJ	No.
	No.
	No.
	You know what.
	I don't [want to know] –
	No.

44

JOY   Okay.

         '

         You wanted to see me.

EJ   Yeah.

         I dunno.

         Maybe that was [a mistake] –

         '

JOY   I'm sorry.

EJ   For what?

JOY   That this is hard.

         '

         And that I can't give you –

         What you [want] –

EJ   You could.

JOY   No.

EJ   Yes.

JOY   No, EJ.

         '

EJ   No.

         You could.

         You could.

         If you tried.

         Only if you tried.

         Because –

45

I'm trying.

I am trying.

'

And you're not –

You're not doing anything.

So.

'

JOY   Okay.

EJ   'Okay.'

JOY   I'm sorry.

'

I think –

I think –

I don't know –

I'm sorry –

But I think that maybe –

Love sometimes doesn't look the way / you think
it might

EJ   No.

No.

No.

No.

Don't do that.

I really [can't] –

Please don't do that.

I really don't want that.

Okay?

'

JOY   I dream about the tree, you know.

Still.

It feels like it's blooming in the centre of my body.

EJ   Stop it.

JOY   I found a bird's nest in its branches one night.

Before I was pregnant.

Tiny –

But it was there.

EJ   Don't do that.

JOY   Three baby birds.

EJ   Please stop it.

JOY   Sticky pink.

EJ   Please.

JOY   Calling for their mother.

EJ   Don't.

Stop that.

Just stop it.

I fucking –

Hate that.

'

You don't get to go back to that.

Hide yourself inside it.

I'm here.

Now.

I am here.

'

Why'd you even come?

'

It is –

So –

Ridiculous –

For me to want –

'

You.

I don't know [you] –

And it feels like there's this –

This –

Creature –

Inside my body –

And it's screaming out –

And clawing out my insides –

And throwing a tantrum –

For someone I don't even [know] –

'

There's nothing [you can do] –

Is there?

Nothing you can [say] –

None of it will [make it okay] –

'

Okay.

She stands straighter.

Yeah.

Okay.

She leaves the stage. Maybe slowly, maybe quickly. JOY watches after her. EJ doesn't come back. JOY waits. Still nothing. She isn't coming back. This should take as long as it takes. When JOY speaks, finally, she speaks to nobody.

JOY   I dream about the tree.

I feel it bloom right in the centre of my body.

There was a bird's nest there.

Before I was pregnant.

Tiny. Delicately twisting.

Three baby birds.

All calling out for their mother.

Sticky pink.

I don't know what kind of birds they were.

Never been good with that sort of thing.

And one morning I went out.

And I stood in the sunlight and I closed my eyes and I smelled the blossoms.

Thick and fragrant in the air.

And I heard something.

49

A mewling.

One of the baby birds curled at the tree roots.

Cloudy eyes blinking quick.

Body crushed.

Fragile bones rattling.

Barely stirring.

'

And I picked it up –

Gently –

So gently –

And I held it close to my chest so it could hear my heart beating.

And I held it there.

I just –

Held it there.

'

END